BENJAMIN WHITE

SHAKESPEARE SIMPLIFIED

Exploring the Bard's World
for Modern Students

CHAPTER 1

Who was Shakespeare?

Before we get into Shakespeare's plays and poems, let's learn about the man himself. You might be wondering why you're being forced to learn about some writer who lived more than 400 years ago. Well, Shakespeare was a fascinating human, and his world wasn't as different from ours as you might think.

The life of William Shakespeare

William Shakespeare was born in 1564 in Stratford-upon-Avon, a market town about 100 miles from London. Think of it as a busy small town where everyone knows everybody else. His dad, John Shakespeare, was a local businessman who worked with leather and gloves. Historical records suggest that he may have faced legal troubles for dealing in unregulated wool, though this remains unclear.

Young Will attended the local grammar school, where he likely studied for free and learned Latin, Greek and classical literature. These schools were common in Elizabethan England and provided a rigorous education focused on classical texts, though they were not equivalent to modern universities.

At age 18, Shakespeare did something that would get people talking on social media today – he married Anne Hathaway (no, not *that* Anne Hathaway), who was 26 and pregnant. They had three kids: Susanna and twins named Hamnet and Judith. Sadly, Hamnet died at age 11, which might explain why death and grief appear so often in Shakespeare's later plays.

Shakespeare goes to London

Sometime in the late 1580s or early 1590s, Shakespeare left his family in Stratford and moved to London. The exact reasons remain unclear, but historians speculate it may have been to seek work opportunities in the theatre or to escape local disputes. This period is part of the so-called 'lost years', where definitive records of Shakespeare's activities are scarce. Some speculate that Shakespeare worked as a teacher, law clerk or even travelled with a theatre company before his name first appeared in London's theatrical records in 1592.

In London, Shakespeare started working in theatres, probably doing everything from holding horses for the rich theatregoers to acting in plays. He wasn't an overnight success – he worked his way up from the bottom. By the 1590s, he was writing plays and becoming part owner of a theatre company called the Lord Chamberlain's Men (later renamed the King's Men, when King James I became their patron).

Life in Elizabethan England

So, what was life like in Shakespeare's time? Well, let me tell you. Queen Elizabeth I was on the throne (until 1603), and England was going through some major changes:

- London was booming with about 200,000 people, making it one of the largest cities in Europe at the time.
- People were exploring the world and bringing back new foods, ideas and words.

- There was no Netflix (duh!), but there were theatres, markets and public executions. While the executions were meant as a punishment, they drew large crowds due to their dramatic nature.
- No electricity meant that plays were performed during daylight hours.
- No women were allowed to act – female parts were played by young men.

The Globe Theatre: Shakespeare's home

The Globe Theatre was like the Sydney Opera House of its day. Built in 1599, it was a massive open-air theatre that could hold up to 3,000 people. If you paid one penny, you could stand in front of the stage; if you paid two or three pennies, then you could sit in the covered seats. Shakespeare's plays weren't just for the rich – they were for everyone.

The original Globe Theatre, built using timber from a previous theatre, had a distinctive round shape with an open roof. After it was destroyed by a fire in 1613 during a performance of *Henry VIII*, it was rebuilt in 1614, maintaining its iconic design.

The Globe Theatre's unique open-air structure significantly influenced Shakespeare's plays, which relied heavily on natural lighting and audience interaction. Its design allowed for an immersive experience, with 'groundlings' standing close to the stage and wealthier patrons seated in the covered galleries.

Why Shakespeare still matters

Now, no doubt you're reading this book because your English teacher is making your class study one of Shakespeare's plays. You're probably asking yourself, 'why bother with this old dead man's work?' Well, Shakespeare was the equivalent of a blockbuster creator in his time – crafting entertainment that appealed to audiences from royalty to commoners. His plays offered something for everyone: thrilling sword fights, witty bants, romance and reflections on human nature.

But what's really important is: Shakespeare wrote about things that still matter today. The themes in his work remain universal and timeless. Love, jealousy, family drama, ambition and friendship are emotions and conflicts that resonate as deeply today as they did 400 years ago, making his plays relatable across generations.

> ### Shakespeare – fast facts
> - Wrote about 37 plays and 154 sonnets
> - Invented more than 1,700 common words we still use today
> - Died on 23 April 1616 (supposedly his birthday!)
> - We don't exactly know what he looked like – there were no selfies back then
> - Many of his plays were never published during his lifetime

Remember, Shakespeare wasn't some boring old writer who wrote boring old plays. He was a creative genius who wrote entertaining stories full of action, romance and humour. In the next chapters we'll look at his language and stories in ways that make sense.

CHAPTER 2

Shakespeare's language

The biggest problem with Shakespeare's plays is the way they are written; the language he uses. It can sometimes feel that when you're reading one of Shakespeare's plays, you're reading an entirely different language. In a way, that's true. But don't stress – we're going to break it all down and make it easier to understand.

Old English vs Modern English

Shakespeare didn't write in Old English (the language of *Beowulf*, which is nearly unrecognisable to modern readers). He wrote in Early Modern English, which is the immediate precursor to the language we use today. While it includes some archaic words and structures, it is largely understandable with a little practice.

Why does Shakespeare sound so different?

Shakespeare's language can sound unusual because it often follows different grammatical structures and uses words that have since fallen out of common usage.

1. **Word order:**

    Instead of 'I am going to the shops', Shakespeare might write 'To the shops I go'.

    Modern: 'Where are you going?' Shakespeare: 'Whither goest thou?'

2. **Fancy words that have changed:**
   a. 'Thou' = you
   b. 'Thy' = your
   c. 'Doth' = does
   d. 'Art' = are
   e. 'Tis' = it is
3. **Words we don't use anymore:**
   a. 'Anon' = right away
   b. 'Wherefore' = why (not where – this is why Juliet asks, 'wherefore art thou Romeo?' She's asking *why* he must be Romeo, not *where* he is!)
   c. 'Prithee' = please
   d. 'Hark' = listen

Shakespeare's greatest hits: words he invented

Here's something you may find cool – Shakespeare popularised many words and phrases that were either newly coined or first recorded in his works. While he didn't invent all of them, his plays and poems introduced these terms to a wider audience.

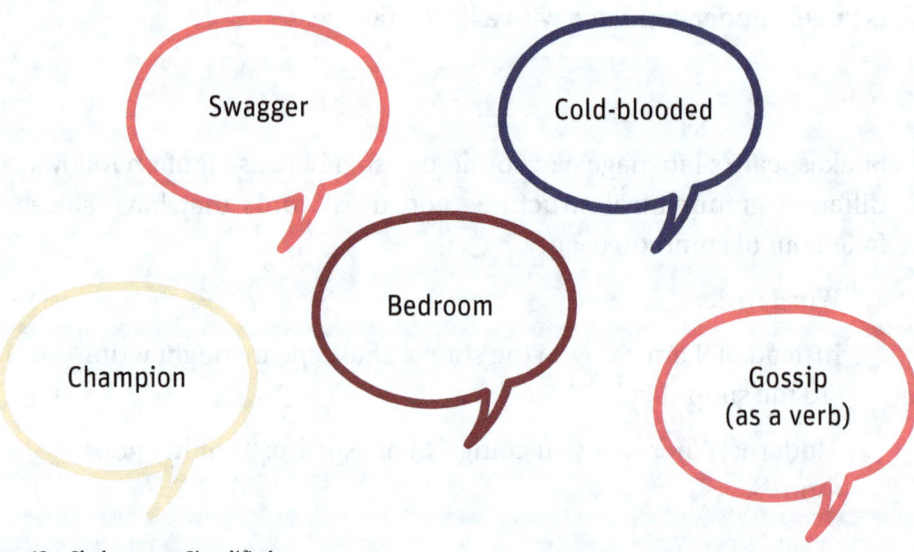

The poetry bit: iambic what-ameter?

Right, now here's the part that might show up in your English exam – or you can use it in your English essay – *iambic pentameter*. Now, that sounds fancy, and it is (your English teacher would love it if you threw that out in class!), but it's relatively simple to get your head (and your heart) around.

First, let's split up these words so you can start to understand it:

- **Iambic:** a pattern of unstressed and stressed syllables
- **Penta:** means five
- **Meter:** the rhythm pattern

Iambic pentameter refers to a line of verse consisting of five pairs of alternating unstressed and stressed syllables, often compared to the rhythm of a heartbeat: da-DUM da-DUM da-DUM da-DUM da-DUM. This rhythm gives Shakespeare's language a natural and flowing quality, even when dealing with complex emotions.

Let's map it out

Take this famous line from *Romeo and Juliet*:

But SOFT | what LIGHT | through YON | der WIN | dow BREAKS

Or try this one from *Macbeth*:

When SHALL | we THREE | meet A | gain in THUN | der, LIGHT | ning, RAIN?

Why did Shakespeare write in this way? Shakespeare used iambic pentameter because it closely mirrors the natural rhythm of spoken English, making it easier for actors to memorise and perform. It also provides a musical quality that draws the audience's attention to key moments in the play. So, there is some method to this madness.

Tips for reading Shakespeare

1. **Don't get hung up on every word.** Focus on the overall meaning of the passage rather than every individual word. Shakespeare's language becomes more accessible as you recognise patterns and key themes.

2. **Watch for puns.** Shakespeare loved a good joke – especially rude ones! Shakespeare's use of puns, double meaning and clever wordplay often adds humour or depth. Keep an eye out for these moments, even if they don't immediately seem funny by modern standards.

3. **Use context clues.** Look at what's happening in the scene. Pay attention to the actions, stage directions and emotions of the characters to help decode their words. For instance, an angry character brandishing a sword likely isn't discussing small matters.

4. **Read aloud.** Shakespeare's plays were written to be performed. Reading lines aloud can help you grasp the rhythm and emotion. Even if you feel silly, this can make the text come alive and improve comprehension.

5. **Use modern tools.** Watching performances or using online resources like annotated editions or video summaries can help your understanding. Hearing actors perform lines will help clarify meanings.

Quick reference guide: common Shakespeare phrases

Modern English	Shakespeare's English	Explanation
Whatever!	As you like it!	Used to express indifference
OMG!	O heavens!	Exclaims surprise or disbelief
No way!	In truth?!	Expresses disbelief, like how it's used in Modern English
Goodbye!	Fare thee well!	A common farewell
Wait a minute!	Stay thy hand!	Asking someone to pause or stop

These translations give a glimpse into the flavour of Shakespeare's language. While the phrases may sound formal or old-fashioned, they reflect the poetic and expressive style of Early Modern English.

Practice makes perfect

Use these phrases to practise speaking like a Shakespeare character. Try substituting them in your everyday conversations for fun and to build your familiarity with the language.

Activity: Shakespeare language toolkit

Learning intention:

By the end of this activity, you will be able to:

- Identify and use Early Modern English vocabulary in context
- Create and recognise iambic pentameter in written text
- Transform modern English into Shakespeare-style language

Your task:

Create your own Shakespeare language passport by completing the following challenges. For each challenge you complete, you'll earn a virtual 'stamp' to showcase your mastery of Shakespearean language.

What you'll need:

- Paper or digital document
- A copy of this chapter (for reference)
- Your brain
- Optional: coloured pens, creativity and a sense of humour

The challenges:

Level 1: Word detective

- Find five modern words we use today that were covered in this chapter.
- Write what each meant in Shakespeare's time.
- Use each word in a modern sentence, for example:
  - *Word:* Gossip
  - *Shakespeare's use:* A verb meaning to be a godparent
  - *Modern use:* My friends always gossip about what happens at school

Level 2: Rhythm master

1. Choose three objects in your room.
2. Write one descriptive line in iambic pentameter for each for example:
   a. My PHONE | lies DARK | upON | the WOOD | en DESK
3. Try this with each of the three objects.

Level 3: Translation time

Take these everyday phrases and make them Shakespearean:

1. I forgot to set my alarm (Shakespearean: 'I did neglect to wind my clock').
2. The Wi-Fi isn't working.
3. I'm going to get pizza (remember to use thy/thou/thine).

Level 4: Create your own

Write a short conversation between:

- You and your phone when it's at 1% battery; or
- You and your homework when it's due tomorrow; or
- You and your breakfast when you're running late.

Write it twice:

1. In Modern English
2. In Shakespeare-style English

CHAPTER 3

Big ideas in Shakespeare's plays

You know how Netflix suggests shows based on themes like 'Drama with Strong Female Leads' or 'Stories about Revenge'? Well, Shakespeare was doing that way before streaming existed. Let's look at the big ideas that pop up in his plays again and again.

Love and situationships/relationships

Shakespeare knew that love isn't just about heart-eyed emojis. His plays show all kinds of relationships. Shakespeare explored love in all its complexities, far beyond simple romantic ideals. His plays examine different types of relationships, from passionate romance to complicated family dynamics and enduring friendships.

Romantic love

- *Romeo and Juliet*: Young love vs family pressure
- *Much Ado About Nothing*: When your mates try to set you up
- *A Midsummer Night's Dream*: Four teenagers in a messy love square

Family love

- *King Lear*: When parents play favourites
- *Hamlet*: Complex family dynamics
- *The Tempest*: Single dad trying his best

Friendship

- *Othello*: Toxic friendships and manipulation
- *Two Gentlemen of Verona*: When your bestie betrays you
- *As You Like It*: Friends who stick together through tough times

Power and ambition

Power corrupts – this is one of Shakespeare's favourite themes to explore. Consider *Macbeth*, where unchecked ambition drives the title character to seize power at all costs. This theme resonates in stories of modern political scandals or corporate greed, illustrating how ambition without limits can spiral into chaos.

Types of power plays

- Getting power: *Macbeth*
- Keeping power: *Richard III*
- Losing power: *Julius Caesar*
- Fighting over power: *Henry V*

Key messages about power

- Power can corrupt good people.
- Being ambitious isn't always bad, but it needs limits.
- Leaders should care about their people, not just their crown.

> ### Mini theme study: *Macbeth*
>
> Picture this: Macbeth is a respected soldier who learns he might become king. This prediction messes with his head – kind of like when someone says you're going to win something, and then you can't think about anything else. His ambition takes over, leading him to:
>
> 1. Murder the king
> 2. Kill his best mate
> 3. Become so paranoid he trusts nobody
> 4. Eventually lose everything
>
> **Think about it:**
>
> Have you ever wanted something so badly you'd do almost anything to get it? Where would you draw the line?

Things aren't always what they seem

Shakespeare loved playing with the idea that appearances can be deceiving. This theme runs through many of his plays in different ways. His plays challenge us to question the surface and look for hidden motivations or realities.

In *Twelfth Night*, a girl named Viola dresses as a boy to get a job but ends up in a love triangle. It's like having a fake social media profile that gets you into complicated situations. *Macbeth* takes this idea even further with the famous line 'Fair is foul, and foul is fair'. Which, translated, means that things that look good might be bad, and things that look bad might be good. Think about how filtered photos on Instagram or carefully curated social media posts might not tell the whole story.

Modern connections

Let's look at just how timeless Shakespeare's themes are, by considering how they pop up in our world:

Shakespeare's theme	Modern example
Forbidden love	Dating someone your parents don't approve of
Power struggles	Competition for school captain
Appearance vs reality	Social media vs real life
Family conflict	Arguing about screen time

The big questions Shakespeare asks

Shakespeare's plays don't just entertain – they make us think about big questions that are still relevant today:

- Is it better to follow your heart or your head?
- How far would you go to achieve your goals?
- Can you trust what you see?
- What makes a good leader?

These questions invite us to reflect on our own lives. For instance, when faced with ethical dilemmas or challenging decisions, we might find parallels with Hamlet's indecision or Macbeth's ambition.

Activity: Theme tracker

Learning intention:

By the end of this activity, you will be able to:

- Identify Shakespeare's major themes in modern media and your own life.
- Make meaningful connections between classical and contemporary storytelling.
- Analyse how universal themes appear in different contexts.

Your task:

For one week, observe your daily life, media consumption and interactions to identify how Shakespearean themes appear. Consider:

- TV shows or movies you watch
- Social media content
- Things that happen in school
- Family situations
- News stories

Theme tracking table

Create a table like this in your notebook or on your device:

Theme	Where I spotted it	What happened
Power	School captain election	Two candidates promised things that they couldn't deliver
Love vs duty	Friend's Instagram post	Friend missed family event for a party
Appearance vs reality	TikTok video	Behind the scenes of a 'perfect' photo or video

Tracking tips:

1. Look for these moments:

    a. **Power struggles:** People competing for influence or leadership, like in debates, elections or sports.

    b. **Conflicts in love:** Tensions between romantic relationships and responsibilities, or unrequited love.

    c. **Deception and misunderstanding:** Times when people misjudge situations or others intentionally mislead them.

    d. **Family and friendships:** Moments of support, betrayal or loyalty within close relationships.

Reflection:

At the end of the week, review your table and reflect:

- Which themes were most common?
- How did they connect to Shakespeare's ideas?
- Were there any moments that were surprising or particularly relatable?

CHAPTER 4

Shakespeare's comedies

If movies were around in Shakespeare's time, he'd be writing romantic comedies. His comedies were the original romcom – full of love stories, mix-ups and laughs. Sure, some of the jokes are seriously old, but the stories still work today.

> **"The course of true love never did run smooth"**
> *A Midsummer Night's Dream*

What makes a Shakespeare comedy?

Shakespeare's comedies blend romantic entanglements, mistaken identities and humorous misunderstandings with moments of slapstick and witty dialogue. They follow a formula designed to entertain while resolving conflicts with harmony and celebration. It goes something like this:

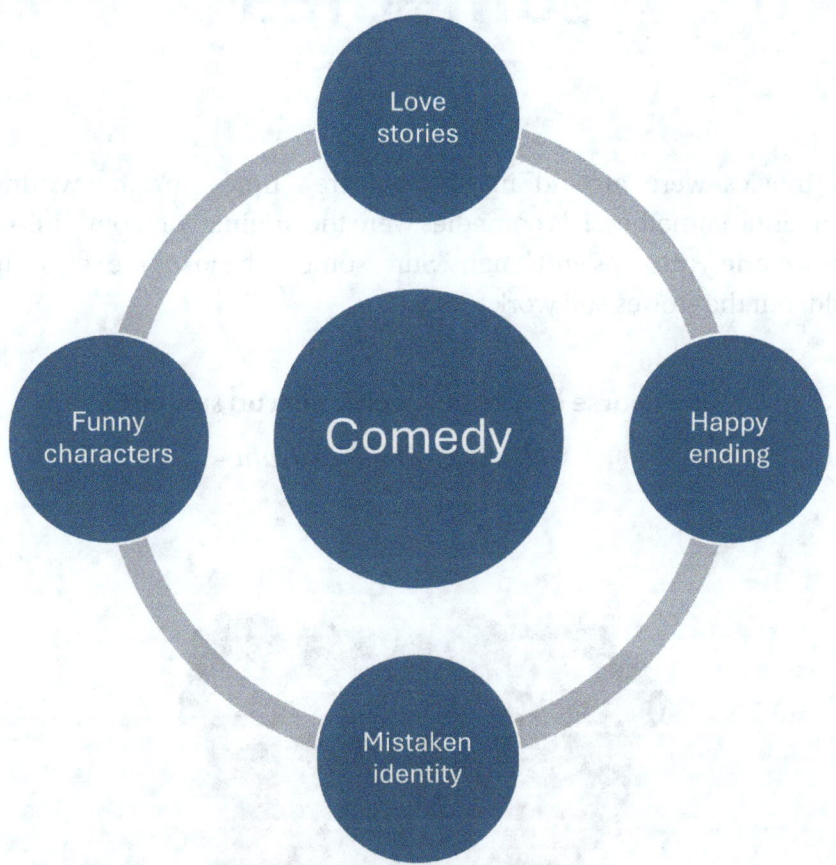

Common plot elements

Shakespeare's comedies often follow this structure:

1. **The problem:** The story begins with a conflict or obstacle, such as a feud, mistaken identity or romantic misunderstanding.

2. **The escape:** Characters leave a familiar setting (often the city) for a magical or natural environment, like the forest in *A Midsummer Night's Dream*.
3. **The chaos:** The story unfolds with misunderstandings, disguises and humorous twists.
4. **The resolution:** The confusion is untangled, and the play ends with reconciliation, forgiveness and often a wedding or celebration.

Case study: *Much Ado About Nothing* trick scene

The set-up: Benedick and Beatrice are two people who claim to hate each other. Their friends know better.

The scene: The Garden Trick

- Benedick's friends know he's hiding in the garden.
- They loudly discuss how Beatrice is madly in love with him.
- Benedick falls for it completely.
- The same trick is played on Beatrice.
- Both go from 'enemies' to 'in love'.

Key quote:

"I do love nothing in the world so well as you: is not that strange?"

(Translation: You're the only person I've ever liked – weird, right?)

Why it works:

The audience knows it's a trick, but the characters don't. This dramatic irony creates the humour.

Types of Shakespearean comedy

Shakespeare wrote different types of comedies:

Type	Example	Modern equivalent
Romantic	*A Midsummer Night's Dream*	Romcom
Problem	*The Merchant of Venice*	Drama with jokes
Mistaken identity	*Twelfth Night*	Body-swap movies

Common comedy characters

Every Shakespeare comedy has these types of characters:

- The lovers (usually more than one couple)
- The clown (for laughs)
- The blocking figure (someone causing problems)
- The wise fool (seems silly but speaks truth)

Language box: Comedy edition

Shakespeare's word	Meaning	Example
Wherefore	Why	Wherefore are thou Romeo?
Marry	Indeed	Marry, you're right!
Prithee	Please	Prithee, be quiet!

Shakespeare's greatest comedy hits

Shakespeare wrote around 17 comedies in total, but there are a few that really stand out. These plays have been performed thousands of times, turned into movies and inspired countless modern stories. Here are three of his most famous comedies that still have audiences laughing and cheering today (no doubt you're studying one of these in class right now):

A Midsummer Night's Dream
- Four young lovers running away
- Mischievous fairies causing chaos
- A guy who gets turned into a donkey
- Love potions gone wrong

Twelfth Night
- Viola pretends to be a boy named Cesario
- She falls for her boss, Duke Orsino
- Olivia falls for Cesario (who's really Viola)
- Everyone's confused until the big reveal

As You Like It
- Characters escape to the magical Forest of Arden
- More disguises (of course!)
- Love notes on trees
- The usual happy ending

Activity: Comedy creator challenge

Learning intention:

By the end of this activity, you will be able to:

- Identify key elements of Shakespearean comedy.
- Create modern versions of comedy scenarios.
- Apply Shakespeare's comedy techniques to a contemporary situation.

Your task: Create your own Shakespeare-style comedy scene

Step 1: Plan your comedy elements

Choose at least three elements from Shakespeare's comedy formula:

- Mistaken identity (i.e. a student is mistaken for the principal during an online class)
- Love triangle/square
- City folk in nature
- Characters in disguise
- Misunderstandings
- Trickery or pranks
- Clever servants
- Happy ending

Step 2: Modern setting

Choose a setting that works for your story:

- Your school
- A music festival
- Social media
- A sports carnival
- School camp
- Shopping centre

Step 3: Create your characters

Develop three or four main characters:

1. Character name
2. Personality
3. What they want
4. Their main problem

Step 4: Write your scene

Follow this structure:

1. The set-up – what's the initial situation?
2. The problem – what goes wrong?
3. The confusion – how does it get worse?
4. The resolution – how does it work out?

CHAPTER 5

Shakespeare's tragedies

When we say something is 'tragic' today, we usually mean it's sad. But Shakespeare's tragedies are more than just sad stories – they're powerful tales about how pride, ambition, jealousy or love can lead to disaster.

> **"These violent delights have violent ends"**
> *Romeo and Juliet*

What makes a tragedy?

Shakespeare's tragedies are more than just sad stories; they explore profound human flaws and their consequences. While they often end in death, the journey focuses on how a hero's tragic flaw (or hamartia) leads to their downfall. Shakespeare's tragedies follow a structure that looks like this:

1. **A noble hero:** The protagonist is often of high status or great potential.
2. **A fatal flaw:** The hero possesses a flaw like ambition, jealousy or indecision that drives the action.

3. **A series of poor choices:** The hero's decisions based on this flaw lead to conflict.
4. **A climactic downfall:** The story reaches a tragic conclusion, where the hero recognises their errors but too late to change their fate.

Theme study: Jealousy in *Othello*

Othello shows how unchecked jealousy can corrode trust and destroy lives. The character of Iago (pronounced *ee-AH-go*) manipulates Othello, planting seeds of doubt and twisting his perception of reality. This theme resonates today, where social media can amplify insecurities and misunderstandings, leading to similar spirals of jealousy.

The spiral of jealousy

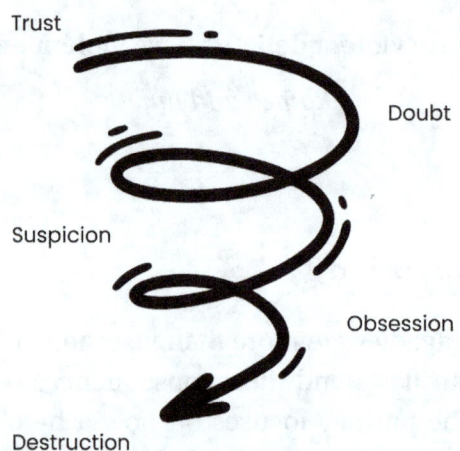

Key quote:

"O, beware, my lord, of jealousy;

It is the green-eyed monster which doth mock

The mate it feeds on"

(Translation: Watch out for jealousy – it's like a monster that plays with its food before eating it.)

Shakespeare's greatest tragic hits

While Shakespeare wrote about 10 tragedies, there are three that have truly stood the test of time. These plays deal with themes that still grab our attention today – love, murder, revenge and ambition. Even if you've never seen these plays, you probably know something about them. They've been turned into movies, inspired TV shows and their stories have been retold countless times. Let's look at three of Shakespeare's most famous tragedies:

Othello
- The ultimate tragedy of jealousy and betrayal:
  - Manipulation and deceit
  - Mistrust in relationships
  - The destructive power of jealousy
  - Tragic consequences of believing lies

Macbeth
- A story about ambition gone wrong:
  - Supernatural elements (witches!)
  - Murder
  - Guilt
  - Madness
  - Power corrupting

Hamlet
- Family drama turned up to 11:
  - Ghost dad
  - Murder mystery
  - Revenge
  - 'To be or not to be'
  - Philosophy mixed with action

Tragic characters you'll meet

Shakespeare knew that a great tragedy needs the right mix of characters. It's like a recipe – you need specific ingredients to make it work. Just as today's hit TV shows have main characters, villains and supporting roles that all serve a purpose, Shakespeare created certain character types that appear across his tragedies. Each plays a crucial part in the story's journey from hope to disaster. Let's meet the key players you'll find in almost every Shakespearean tragedy:

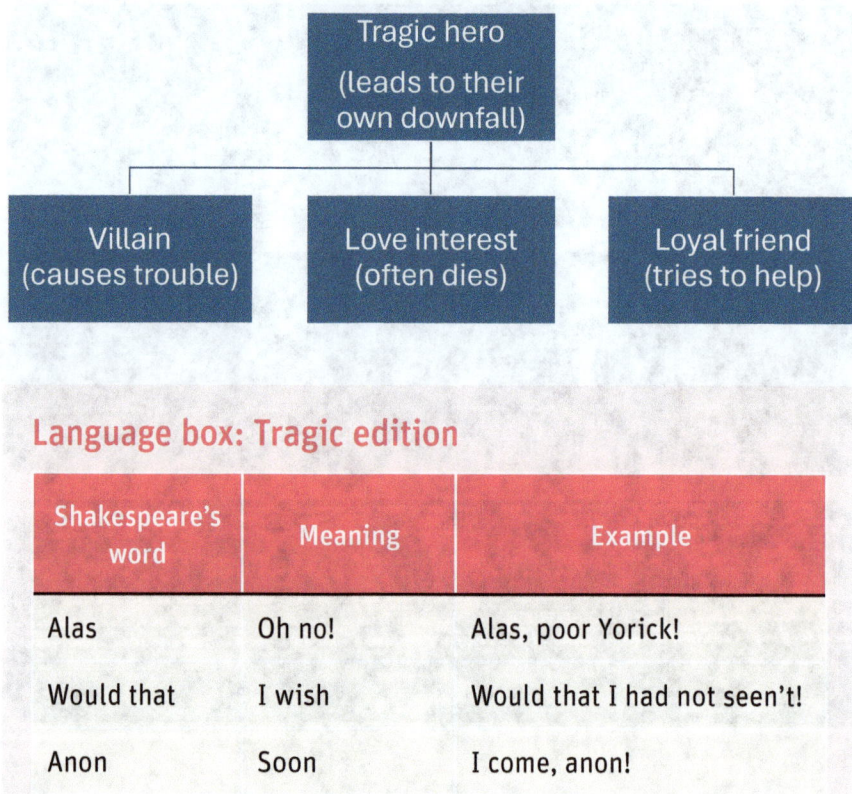

Language box: Tragic edition

Shakespeare's word	Meaning	Example
Alas	Oh no!	Alas, poor Yorick!
Would that	I wish	Would that I had not seen't!
Anon	Soon	I come, anon!

Why tragedies still matter

Shakespeare's tragedies weren't just written to make audiences cry – they were written to make us think about human nature and the consequences of our actions. These plays still grab our attention today because they show us truths about ourselves that haven't changed in 400 years.

Power and its problems
- A social media influencer who'll do anything for more followers
- A sports star who cheats to stay on top
- A politician who breaks promises to keep power
- A student leader who forgets their friends after becoming school captain

Pride before a fall
- The star athlete who won't listen to their coach
- The student who won't ask for help until it's too late
- The friend who can't admit they were wrong
- The leader who won't change their mind even when they should

When emotions take over
- Othello's jealousy ---> Like obsessively checking your partner's DMs
- Romeo and Juliet's rush into love ---> Like making huge decisions based on feelings without thinking
- Hamlet's grief and anger ---> Like letting emotions build up until they explode

Modern-day tragedies

Ever noticed how some news stories feel like they could be Shakespeare plays? Whether it's in the headlines or happening in your own school, Shakespeare's tragic patterns keep showing up. These modern examples prove that his understanding of human nature – our mistakes, our pride, our big feelings – was spot on. Even though he wrote these plays centuries ago, we can spot his tragic themes playing out in both major world events and everyday life:

Real-life stories	In your world
• Celebrity scandals and downfalls • Sports stars losing everything through bad choices • Business leaders whose greed leads to disaster • Political leaders brought down by pride	• Friendship groups torn apart by jealousy • Reputations ruined by social media posts (getting cancelled!) • Relationships destroyed by lack of trust • Teams failing because of one person's ego

The big lessons

Shakespeare's tragedies aren't just entertainment – they're like an ancient version of 'life lessons from people who stuffed up!' Each tragic hero learns something important, but unfortunately for them, they figure it out too late. Luckily for us, we can learn from their mistakes!

Shakespeare's tragedies teach us to:

♦ Think before acting

♦ Control our emotions

♦ Be careful what we wish for

♦ Listen to good advice

♦ Know ourselves better

Activity: Modern tragedy analysis

Learning intention:

By the end of this activity, you will be able to:

- Identify key elements of a Shakespearean tragedy
- Analyse how tragic flaws lead to consequences
- Connect classical tragic themes to a modern situation

Your task:

Step 1: Choose your subject

Pick ONE of these options:

1. A famous person who experienced a downfall
2. A character from a movie/TV show with a tragic story
3. A character from a book/game who faces tragedy
4. Create your own tragic character

Step 2: Tragic character profile

Complete the Character Analysis Worksheet (Appendix 1).

Step 3: Map their downfall

Create a timeline showing:

1. Starting position (what makes them great?)
2. Warning signs (what hints of trouble appear?)
3. Crisis point (what major event changes everything?)
4. Downfall (what are the consequences?)
5. Realisation (what do they learn too late?)

Step 4: Shakespeare connection

Which Shakespearean tragedy does your story most resemble?

- *Macbeth* (ambition)
- *Othello* (jealousy)
- *Hamlet* (indecision)
- *Romeo and Juliet* (rushed decisions)

Step 5: Modern twist

Explain how this story could happen today:

- What would be different?
- What would be the same?
- How would social media play a role?
- What advice would you give the character?

Extension:

1. Write a dramatic monologue for your character.
2. Create a social media feed showing their downfall.
3. Draw a comic strip of key moments.
4. Write an alternative ending where they learn their lesson in time.

CHAPTER 6

Shakespeare's histories

Ever wondered what Netflix would have looked like in Tudor England? Shakespeare's history plays were like the original historical dramas – full of power, politics and plenty of drama. But unlike *The Crown*, these plays were written close to when the actual events happened!

"Uneasy lies the head that wears the crown"
Henry IV, Part 2

What makes a history play?

Shakespeare's history plays blend elements of historical fact with dramatic storytelling, creating a mix of political intrigue, family drama and epic battles. They explore the lives of English monarchs and the consequences of their actions on the nation's future. Let's break down what makes these plays different from comedies and tragedies:

Based on real events

- Unlike his other plays, Shakespeare got these stories from:
  - Historical records
  - Stories passed down
  - Chronicles (history books of the time)
  - Recent events (some were like writing about your grandparents' time)

Politics and power

- These plays show us:
  - How kings gain power
  - How they lose power
  - Who supports them
  - Who betrays them
  - What happens to the country during political chaos

Leadership lessons

- Shakespeare explores big questions about leadership:
  - Does being born royal automatically make you a good leader?
  - Is it better to be loved or feared?
  - Should a leader follow their head or their heart?
  - How do you get people to follow you?
  - What happens when leaders make bad choices?

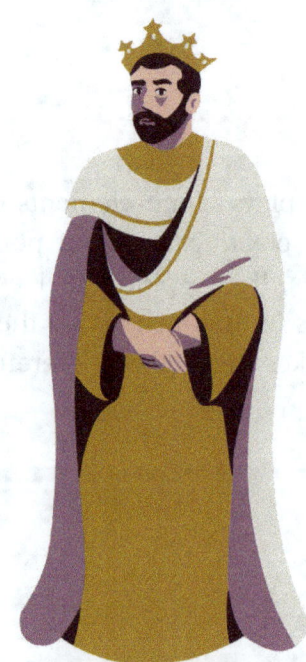

The connected story

Imagine the most epic TV series ever. Shakespeare's histories are like that – they're all connected. They're kind of like the MCU's multiverse. The original multiverse of madness. Shakespeare's histories show:

♦ How one king's actions affect the next
♦ Family drama across generations
♦ Old grudges leading to new conflicts
♦ Characters appearing in multiple plays
♦ Actions having consequences years later

Let's map this out, so we can all get our heads around it:

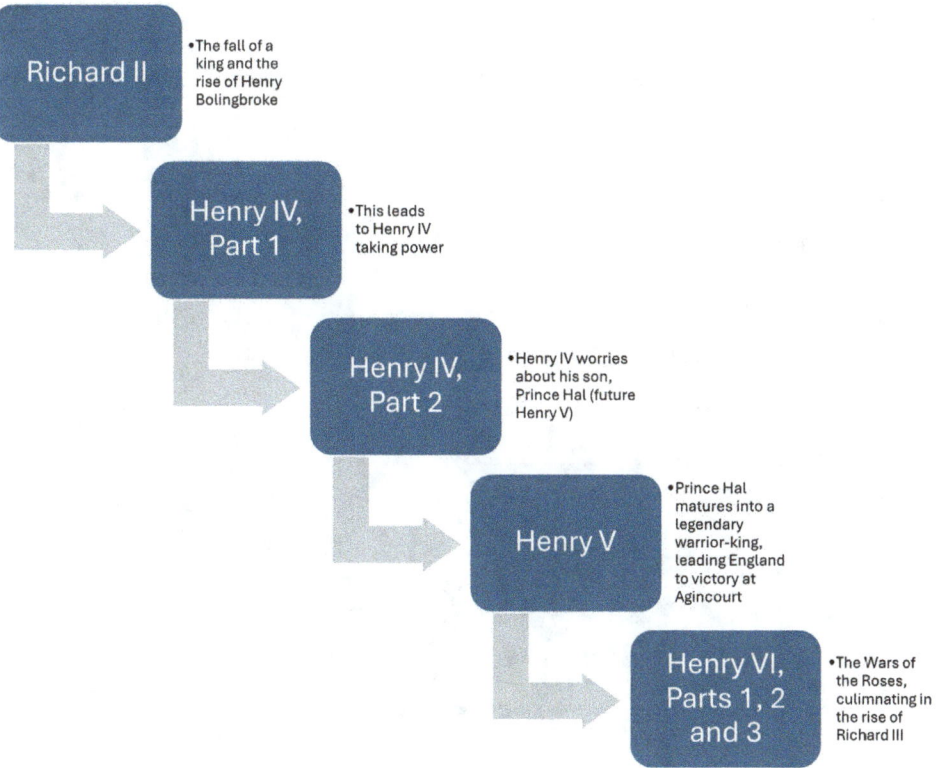

Shakespeare's histories **41**

Case study: *Henry V*

Henry V is probably Shakespeare's most famous history play. It's about a young king who needs to prove himself as a leader.

The story:

Young Henry used to hang out with a bad crowd in the pubs. When he becomes king, everyone doubts him. But he:

- Steps up to the challenge
- Unites his people
- Leads them to victory against France
- Proves everyone wrong

Key quote:

"Once more unto the breach, dear friends, once more!"

(Translation: Come on team, let's give it another go!)

Key themes:

- Leadership
- Growing up
- National pride
- Proving yourself

'Based on a true story'

Shakespeare dramatised historical events to captivate his audience. While his plays are inspired by history, he often altered details for dramatic effect, creating villains, heroes and conflicts that heightened the emotional impact. Let's see how he balanced fact and fiction...

What Shakespeare changed

Made characters more dramatic

- Real Richard III: Probably not as evil as Shakespeare made him.
  - Shakespeare's Richard III: A villain who literally tells the audience he's going to be bad.
- Real Hotspur: An experienced soldier in his 40s.
  - Shakespeare's Hotspur: A young, hot-headed warrior who makes a perfect rival for Prince Hal.

Simplified complex events

- Real Wars of the Roses: Complicated political mess lasting 30 years.
  - Shakespeare's version: Clear good guys and bad guys, exciting battles.
- Real politics: Lots of boring meetings and paperwork.
  - Shakespeare's politics: Dramatic confrontations and murder plots.

Adding exciting speeches
- Real battles: Probably not much talking.
  - Shakespeare's battles: Epic speeches that we still quote today.
    - "Once more unto the breach, dear friends!" (*Henry V*)
    - "Now is the winter of our discontent." (*Richard III*)
- Added dramatic scenes that never happened.
  - Henry V walking around his camp in disguise.
  - Richard III being haunted by ghosts.

Created better villains
- Made bad guys more obviously evil
- Added dramatic death scenes
- Created interesting motives
- Added personal revenge plots

What he kept real

Major historical events
- The Battle of Agincourt
- The Wars of the Roses
- The murder of the Princes in the Tower
- Richard II's overthrow

Key battles and deaths
- Who fought whom
- Who won
- Who died
- Where battles happened

Order of monarchs
- Kept the basic timeline accurate
- Showed how the crown passed from king to king
- Maintained family relationships
- Kept track of who had the better claim to rule

Basic political conflicts
- England vs France rivalry
- York vs Lancaster feud
- Church vs state tensions
- Nobles vs king power struggles

Language box: The histories

Shakespeare's word	Meaning	Example
Crown	Kingdom/power	For the crown of France
Realm	Country	This blessed realm
Usurp	Take power illegally	Usurp the crown

Why these plays matter today

You might be thinking, 'Why should I care about plays about old English kings?' Well, fair enough! Even though these plays were written more than 400 years ago about even older events, they deal with issues that are quite familiar. Especially in our unpredictable world.

These plays show us that people haven't really changed – we still deal with the same big questions about leadership, powers and responsibility. Let's look at what these old stories can teach us about modern life:

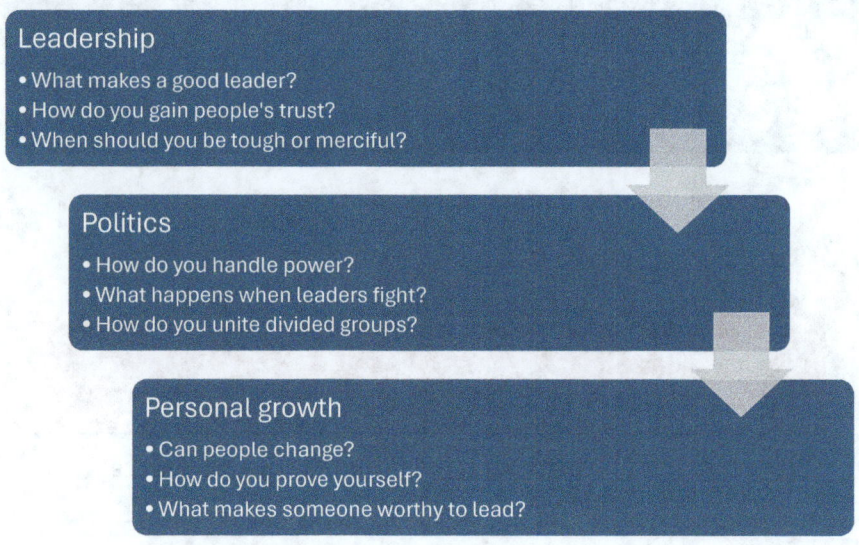

Activity: Shakespeare's histories – fact vs fiction

Learning intention:

By the end of this activity, you will be able to:

- Analyse how Shakespeare transforms history into drama
- Identify historical and dramatic elements in plays
- Evaluate the effectiveness of dramatic choices in historical storytelling

Your task:

Step 1: Compare and contrast

Select one of Shakespeare's history plays, like *Henry V* or *Richard III*. Complete the Historical Analysis Worksheet (Appendix 2).

Step 2: Dramatic techniques analysis

Find examples of how Shakespeare uses these techniques to make history more dramatic:

1. Speeches and language
   a. Find one famous speech.
   b. Explain what historical event it's based on.
   c. Analyse how Shakespeare made it more dramatic.
2. Character development
   a. Choose one character.
   b. List their historical actions.
   c. Identify what Shakespeare added.
   d. Explain why these changes work dramatically.

3. Historic themes in modern context

    a. Identify one major theme (for example, leadership, power, loyalty).

    b. Find three examples from the play.

    c. Connect them to modern situations.

Step 3: Evaluate dramatic choices

Answer these questions with evidence from the play you're studying:

1. Why did Shakespeare change certain historical facts?

2. How effective were his dramatic choices?

3. What does this play teach us about:

    a. Leadership?

    b. Power?

    c. Human nature?

CHAPTER 7

Shakespeare's sonnets

Love poems have been around forever, but Shakespeare's sonnets are something special. Think of them as the original pop songs – they're about love, jealousy, beauty and time passing. All packed into a tight 14-line format.

> **'Shall I compare thee to a summer's day?'**
> Sonnet 18 (probably Shakespeare's most famous line)

What makes a sonnet?

A sonnet is a highly structured 14-line poem with a specific rhyme scheme and rhythm. Shakespeare's sonnets often explore timeless themes like love, beauty and the passage of time, with a 'twist' or resolution near the end.

Sonnets contain the following elements:

- 14 lines exactly
- Special rhythm pattern (iambic pentameter)
- Special rhyme scheme
- Usually about love or deep thoughts

- Has a twist or turn near the end

The blueprint of a sonnet

Just like architects need blueprints to build houses, Shakespeare followed a specific plan for his sonnets. Here's how a sonnet is built, piece by piece:

First quatrain (4 lines)
- 'Quatrain' means four lines
- Sets up the theme/problem

Second quatrain (4 lines)
- Develops the idea

Third quatrain (4 lines)
- Further develops or changes direction

Couplet (2 lines)
- 'Couplet' means two lines
- The twist/conclusion

Case study: Sonnet 18

Let's have a bit of a closer look at Shakespeare's most famous sonnet – Sonnet 18.

'Shall I compare thee to a summer's day?

Thou art more lovely and more temperate.'

What's happening:

Sonnet 18 highlights Shakespeare's mastery of metaphor and enduring themes:

- **Main idea:** The speaker compares their beloved to a summer's day, finding them superior in beauty.
- **Development:** While summer fades, the beloved's beauty is eternal, preserved through the poem.
- **Twist:** The poem itself ensures the beloved's immortality.

Modern version:

'Should I compare you to a perfect day?

Actually, you're even better than that...'

The big themes in Shakespeare's sonnets

If Shakespeare's sonnets were an album, these would be his greatest hits. While each sonnet tells its own story, certain themes keep coming up – kind of like how modern songs often deal with love, heartbreak and relationships. These themes weren't just relevant in Shakespeare's time; they're the same things we post, tweet, share and talk about today.

Love

Shakespeare's sonnets explore love in all its forms, from the blissful ideas to the painfully complicated. From friendships to situationships. Shakespeare's sonnets cover it all.

- **Perfect love:** Shakespeare often wrote about love as something pure and transcendent. It's an ideal that feels almost too good to be true.
  - Example: In Sonnet 18, the poet compares their beloved to a summer's day, capturing the beauty and perfection of love in eternal poetry.
- **Messy love:** Love isn't always perfect. It's full of flaws, misunderstandings and emotions that can't always be

controlled. Shakespeare shows us how love can be chaotic and deeply human.

- Example: Sonnet 147 compares love to a fever, showing the turmoil it can bring.

♦ **Jealous love:** Shakespeare captures the sting of jealousy, the fear of losing someone, the pain of comparison.

- Example: In Sonnet 61, the poet wonders if their beloved is unfaithful, exploring how jealousy can taint love.

♦ **Forbidden love:** Some of Shakespeare's sonnets hint at love that goes against societal norms or expectations, showing the challenges of loving someone you're not supposed to.

- Example: These themes resonate with ideas of secretive or unaccepted relationships.

Time and beauty

Shakespeare was fascinated by the fleeting nature of beauty and the unstoppable march of time.

♦ **Beauty doesn't last:** Beauty fades as time goes on, and Shakespeare often reflects on how physical attractiveness is only temporary.

- Example: Sonnet 73 uses autumn and winter imagery to show the inevitable decline of youth and beauty.

♦ **Time changes everything:** Relationships, appearances and even memories evolve as time passes.

- Example: In Sonnet 60, Shakespeare compares time to waves, constantly moving forward and wearing things down.

♦ **Memory and poetry preserves:** Even though time changes everything, Shakespeare believed that poetry could capture beauty and keep it alive forever.

- Example: Sonnet 18 ends with the bold claim that the poet's words will make their beloved's beauty eternal.

Truth and lies

The sonnets delve into the tension between appearance and reality, exploring what's true and what's false in relationships.

- **Real vs fake:** Shakespeare questions whether outward appearances reflect inner truths.
  - Example: In Sonnet 138, the poet reflects on mutual deceptions in a relationship, revealing how people sometimes accept lies for the sake of love.

- **Inner beauty vs outer beauty:** True beauty, Shakespeare suggests, lies within a person's character rather than their physical appearance.
  - Example: Sonnet 94 contrasts those who appear beautiful but are morally corrupt with those whose inner beauty shines through.

- **True love vs false love:** Shakespeare often distinguishes between love that's genuine and love that's superficial and self-serving.
  - Example: Sonnet 116 famously defines true love as steadfast and unchanging, even in the face of challenges.

Language box: The sounds of a sonnet

Shakespeare's word	Modern meaning
Thee	You
Thou	You
Thy	Your
Art	Are
Tis	It is

The rhyme scheme

Shakespeare may have been a bit reckless when he was inventing words, just because he couldn't find one to work in his plays. But when it came to his sonnets, he was very particular. A strict 14 lines with a rhyme scheme. They follow this pattern: ABAB CDCD EFEF GG. Sounds complicated? Let's break it down:

What those letters mean

- All lines ending in the same letter rhyme with each other.
- So, all 'A' lines rhyme with each other
- All 'B' lines rhyme with each other
- And so on…

Let's see it in action

Using the first quatrain in Sonnet 18…

Shall I compare thee to a summer's DAY? (A)
Thou art more lovely and more TEMPERATE (B)
Rough winds do shake the darling buds of MAY (A)
And summer's lease hath all too short a DATE (B)

Think of it like a song structure:

1. **Verse 1** (first quatrain – ABAB)
   a. Like the first verse of a song
   b. Sets up what the poem's about
2. **Verse 2** (second quatrain – CDCD)
   a. Like the second verse
   b. Develops the idea with new rhymes

3. **Verse 3** (third quatrain – EFEF)
   a. Like the final verse
   b. Maybe changes direction a bit
4. **The big finish** (couplet – GG)
   a. Like the chorus or hook
   b. The part that sticks in your head
   c. Usually has the biggest punch

> **Pro tip: Reading the sonnets**
>
> When you're reading a sonnet:
> - Read it once to get the story.
> - Read it again, noticing the rhymes.
> - Listen for how the rhymes help emphasise important words.
> - Pay special attention to that final couplet – it's usually the key to the whole poem!

Why sonnets matter today

Shakespeare's sonnets might seem old-fashioned, but they deal with the same stuff we obsess over today. Think about it – we're still writing, singing and posting about love, beauty, jealousy and time passing. The only real difference is the platform!

Love and relationships
- Then: Writing sonnets about secret lovers
- Now: Posting relationship updates on Instagram
- Both: Trying to capture feelings in words

Beauty standards
- Then: Sonnets about ideal beauty vs reality
- Now: Instagram filters and #nofilter posts
- Both: Wrestling with real vs artificial beauty

Time and ageing
- Then: Sonnets about youth fading
- Now: Anti-ageing product ads and #ageinggracefully
- Both: Worrying about getting older

Fun fact!

Shakespeare wrote 154 sonnets, but they weren't all about love – some were about friendship, some about politics and some were just showing of his writing skills!

Activity: Sonnet structure analysis

Learning intention:

By the end of this activity, you will be able to:

♦ Identify and explain the key features of a Shakespearean sonnet

♦ Analyse how form and content work together in sonnets

♦ Understand how themes are developed across the structure

Your task:

Step 1: Structural analysis

Using Sonnet 18 ('Shall I compare thee to a summer's day?'), or the sonnet you are studying in class, complete the Sonnet Analysis Worksheet (Appendix 3).

Step 2: Tracking the themes

1. Identify the main theme(s)

   Love

   Time

   Beauty

   Nature

   Other:

2. Show how the theme develops:

   In the first quatrain:

   In the second quatrain:

   In the third quatrain:

   In the couplet:

Step 3: Language analysis

Find examples of:

1. Metaphor
2. Imagery
3. Contrast
4. Personal pronouns

Extension:

Compare this sonnet's structure with a modern love song of your choice:

- How is it similar?
- How is it different?
- Which is more effective? Why?

Remember: A sonnet is like a puzzle – each piece plays a part in creating the whole.

CHAPTER 8

Analysing Shakespeare's characters

Understanding Shakespeare's characters is like being a detective – you need to gather clues, examine evidence and piece together the full picture. Let's learn how to crack the character code!

> **"All the world's a stage, and all the men and women are merely players"**
>
> *As You Like It*

How to analyse a character

Analysing Shakespeare's characters is like building a profile for a favourite TV or movie character. Pay attention to their words, actions and relationships. Just as you might always analyse or consider why your favourite character in *Stranger Things* or *Heartstopper* makes certain choices, we can break down Shakespeare's characters in the same way.

What to look for:

What they say
- Their actual words (dialogue)
- Their tone (how they say things)
- Their soliloquies (private thoughts)
- What they say to different people
- What they're not saying

What they do
- Their actions (big and small)
- Whether actions match their words
- How they treat others
- Their reactions to events
- Their choices and decisions

What others say about them
- Public opinion of the character
- Private comments about them
- Different perspectives from different characters
- Gossip and rumours
- How they're described when they're not present

How they change
- Their starting point
- Key moments that change them
- Gradual development
- Major turning points
- Where they end up

Their relationships
- Family connections
- Friendships
- Romantic relationships
- Enemies and rivals

Case study: *Hamlet*

Let's look at how to analyse one of Shakespeare's most complex characters:

Character profile: Hamlet

On the surface	Deeper analysis
• Prince of Denmark	• Struggles with duty vs doubt
• University student	• Questions everything
• Son who loses his father	• Uses wit to hide pain
• Asked by ghost to seek revenge	• Relationship with family is complicated
	• Actions have unintended consequences

Key quote:

"To be, or not to be, that is the question."

(Translation: Do I want to keep going or just give up? That's the real question.)

Breaking down character analysis

Just as detectives have specific methods for solving cases, there are proven methods for analysing Shakespeare's characters. Let's look at each technique in detail:

Element to analyse	Example
Words and language choices **Character's speech reveals:** • **Social status (formal vs casual language)** • **Education level (simple vs complex words)** • **Emotional state (calm vs angry language)** • **True feelings (private vs public speech)**	Example: Hamlet's language • Public speech: Clever wordplay, seems mad • Private soliloquies: Deep, philosophical thoughts • What this tells us: He's putting on an act
Actions and decisions Look for: • **Key decisions they make** • **How they treat others** • **Reactions under pressure** • **Differences between public and private behaviour**	Example: Hamlet's actions • Public: Acts strangely, seems unstable • Private: Carefully plans and thinks things through • What this tells us: He's more calculated than he appears

Element to analyse	Example
Relationships and interactions Examine: • Family dynamics • Friendships • Romantic relationships • Power relationships • Treatment of those above/below them socially	**Example: Hamlet's relationship with his mother, Gertrude** • "Frailty, thy name is woman!" • Shows his disappointment and anger • Still seeks her approval • Tries to protect her despite feeling betrayed • Complex mix of love and disgust • What this tells us: His struggle with trust; his moral standards; his emotional complexity; his inability to just hate or love completely
Character development Track how they change through the play: • Starting point • Major turning points • Final position • What causes changes • Impact of events on them	**Example: Hamlet's journey** • Starts: Grieving son • Changes: Seeing ghost, killing Polonius, being sent away • Ends: More decisive, accepts fate • Key change: "Let be" – finally stops overthinking
Context and circumstances Consider what shapes their behaviour: • Their position in society • Time period expectations • Family pressures • Political situation • Personal history	**Example: Hamlet's context** • Prince of Denmark • University student • Son expected to avenge father • Court full of spies • Medieval royal politics

Analysing Shakespeare's characters

Writing about characters

Think of your character analysis like building a strong argument. When analysing characters in Shakespeare's work (or any text you're studying in English), you can follow the **What; How; Why; So** approach to help build and develop your analysis and your argument.

What; How; Why; So

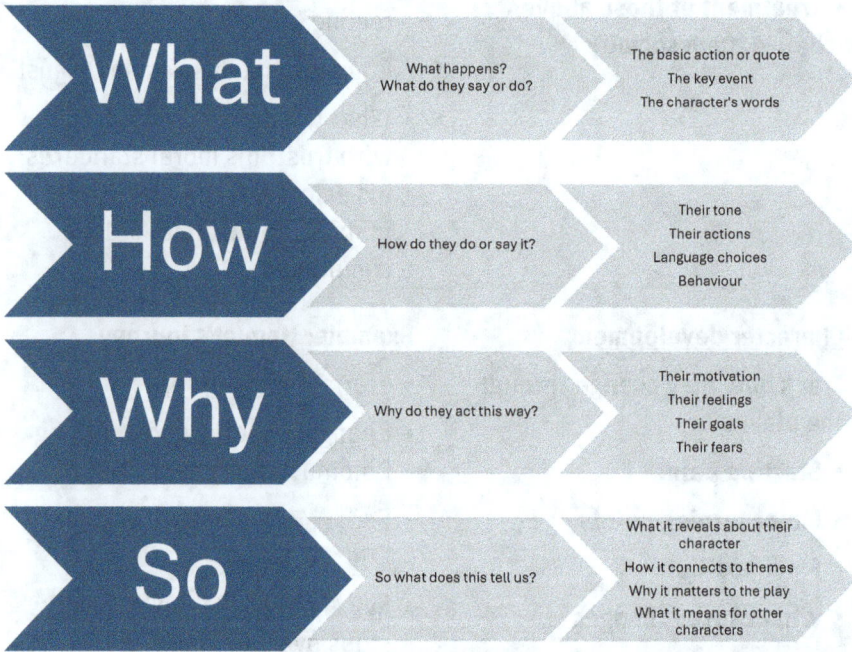

Example using *Macbeth*

1. WHAT: Macbeth kills Duncan.

2. HOW: He does it at night; while Duncan is sleeping; in his own castle; after much hesitation.

3. WHY: Ambitious for power; influenced by his wife; driven by prophecies; afraid of failure.

4. SO: This shows Macbeth's inner conflict; moral weakness; is influenced by others; betrays Duncan's hospitality.

Practice paragraph:

When Macbeth kills Duncan (WHAT), he does it secretly at night while his victim sleeps (HOW). He acts this way because he knows it is wrong, but his ambition overrides his loyalty (WHY). This reveals both his moral awareness and his weakness of character, demonstrating that ambition can corrupt even a noble person (SO).

Common mistakes to avoid

- Don't just describe what happens.
- Analyse why it happens.

- Don't make claims without evidence.
- Support points with quotes.

- Don't ignore contradictions.
- Explore complexity.

- Don't judge by modern standards.
- Consider historical context.

Activity: Shakespeare's character lab

Learning intention:

By the end of this activity, you will be able to:

♦ Apply the What; How; Why; So method to write about characters

♦ Support character analysis with evidence from the text

♦ Make meaningful connections between characters' words, actions and motivations

Your task:

Choose one significant moment from the play you're studying and analyse a character following these steps...

Step 1: Choose your moment

Pick a key scene where your character:

♦ Makes an important decision

♦ Reveals their true feelings

♦ Changes in some way

♦ Interacts with others significantly

Step 2: What; How; Why; So analysis

Complete the What; How; Why; So Analysis Worksheet (Appendix 4).

Step 3: Character development

How does this moment show character development...

Before this moment?

During this moment?

After this moment?

Step 4: Evidence bank

Find TWO quotes from the text that support your analysis.

QUOTE 1

Context:

What it reveals:

QUOTE 2

Context:

What it reveals:

Extension:

Using this key moment, examine it from three different perspectives:

1. From another character's view
2. From a modern perspective
3. From the audience's perspective

Analysing Shakespeare's characters **67**

CHAPTER 9

Adapting and transforming Shakespeare

Ever watched a movie and thought, 'I've seen this before'? Many modern stories are Shakespeare's plays in disguise. Writers, directors and artists keep transforming his work because the core stories are strong and, as we have seen, the themes are universal. Shakespeare's stories work in any time and place.

From page to screen

Whether you're watching a movie, streaming a TV series, or checking out the latest anime, you might be experiencing Shakespeare without even knowing it. His stories have been adapted countless time across different cultures, genres and mediums. Sometimes they're obvious remakes (like *10 Things I Hate About You*) and sometimes they're subtle influences (like *The Lion King*).

Each adaptation changes elements of the original – maybe the setting, time period or style – but keeps the core story and themes that make Shakespeare's work so powerful. When creators adapt Shakespeare, they usually consider the following things:

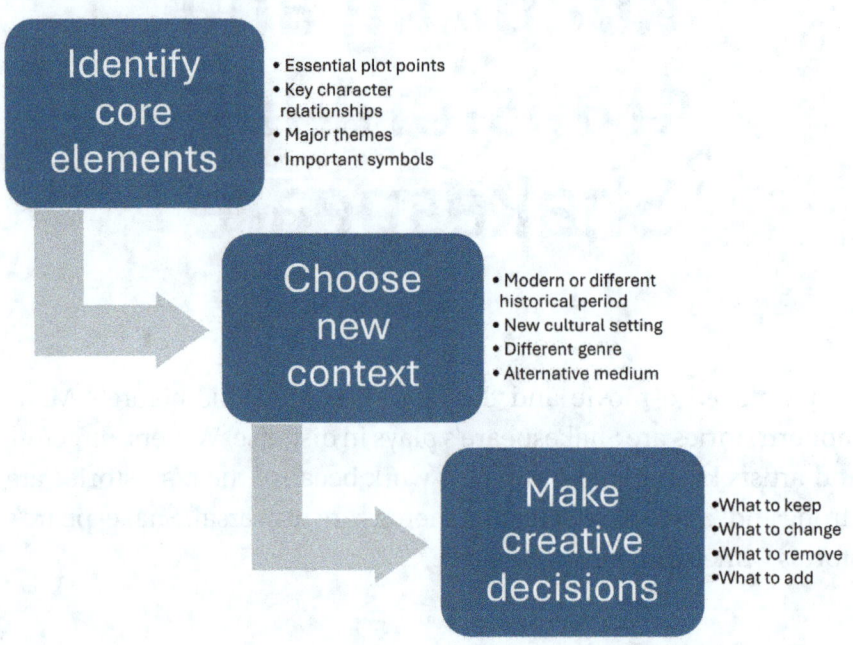

Case study: Transforming *Macbeth*

Let's consider how this process works with different adaptations of *Macbeth*.

Throne of Blood (1957)

Kept: Ambition, prophecy, murder, guilt

Changed: Setting to feudal Japan

Added: Samurai code of honour

Removed: English wordplay and witches

Result: Universal story in Japanese context

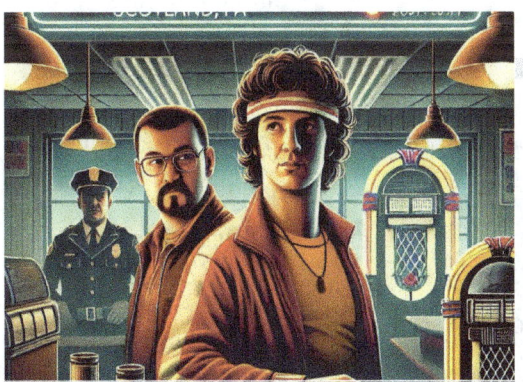

Scotland, PA (2001)

Kept: Power struggle, murder plot

Changed: Castle to fast-food restaurant

Added: Dark humour, 70s setting

Removed: Royal politics

Result: Commentary on American ambition

Adapting and transforming Shakespeare

Types of transformation

Just as there are many ways to tell a story, there are many ways to transform Shakespeare. Directors, writers and artists use different approaches to make his plays speak to modern audiences. Each type of transformation has its own challenges and opportunities, and many adaptations use more than one approach. Let's look at the main ways creators transform Shakespeare's works for new audiences:

Transformation	Process	Example
Update the setting	• Keep original dialogue • Change time/place • Update references • Modify costumes/props	*Romeo + Juliet* (1996) • Verona Beach not Verona • Guns not swords • Cars not horses • Corporate empires not noble houses
Cultural translations	• Adapt to new culture • Change cultural references • Modify social dynamics • Adjust language style	*Omkara* (2006, Indian *Othello*) • Political gangster • Indian caste politics • Traditional waistband as proof • Indian marriage traditions

Transformation	Process	Example
Change the genre	• Identify genre conventions • Map story to new genre • Adjust the tone and style • Add genre-specific elements	*Warm Bodies* (2013, *Romeo and Juliet*) • Zombie apocalypse genre • Supernatural romance • Horror elements added • Comedy tone introduced
Change the medium	• Adapt for new format • Use medium-specific tools • Consider audience expectations • Add new storytelling elements	*She's the Man* (2006, *Twelfth Night*) • Film medium requirements • Visual comedy added • Modern teen movie conventions • Sports subplot expanded
Shift the perspective	• Choose new viewpoint • Expand minor characters • Fill in story gaps • Add new subplots	*Rosencrantz & Guildenstern Are Dead* (1990, characters from *Hamlet*) • Minor characters become leads • Behind-the-scenes story • Philosophical elements added • Comedy increased

Activity: Adaptation analysis

Learning intention:

By the end of this activity, you will be able to:

- Identify how Shakespeare's works are transformed for modern audiences
- Analyse what changes and what stays the same in adaptations
- Evaluate the effectiveness of different adaptation choices

Your task:

Pick ONE film/show from the list at the back of this book (Appendix 5) that adapts the Shakespeare play that you're studying. Complete this analysis:

Original play:

Modern version:

TRANSFORMATION CHECKLIST

Setting: Original:

                    New:

                    Why changed:

Characters: Original name:

                    New name:

                    How changed:

Key scene analysis: Original scene:

How adapted:

Why changed:

What stayed the same:
1.
2.
3.

What changed:
1.
2.
3.

Overall effect: Does it work? Why/why not?

Remember: Good adaptations balance staying true to the Shakespeare story while making it fresh for new audiences!

CHAPTER 10

Tips for reading and enjoying Shakespeare

Reading Shakespeare is like learning a new skill – it gets easier with practice and the right techniques. This final chapter will give you some practical strategies to tackle any Shakespeare play with confidence.

> "The more I read, the more I understand"
>
> Every successful English student, ever.

Case study: Breaking down a speech

Let's look at how to tackle one of Shakespeare's most famous speeches using our key strategies.

The speech:

"Friends, Romans, countrymen, lend me your ears."

– *Julius Caesar*, Act 3, Scene 2

Breaking it down:

1. First read: Just get the vibe
   a. Someone's making a public speech.
   b. They want people to listen.
2. Second read: Look closer
   a. Three types of people are addressed.
   b. Informal to formal order.
   c. "Lend me your ears" = "Listen up!"
3. Third read: Analyse
   a. Builds connections with audience.
   b. Careful word choice.
   c. Persuasive technique.

Essential reading strategies

Before you start	While reading
• Get context from a plot summary • Check character list • Know the type of play • Set up a good study space	• Read aloud • Break into chunks • Look for familiar words • Use modern translations alongside

Taking notes

Just as you might take notes while watching a complicated TV show or reading your novel ("wait, who's related to who again?!"), good notetaking helps you keep track of what's happening in Shakespeare. You don't need to write down everything – focus on the important stuff that will help you follow and understand the story. Here's one way you can organise your notes:

Character notes

Who are they?

What do they want?

Key relationships?

Plot points

What happened?

Why important?

What next?

Language notes

Important quotes

Word meanings

Language patterns

Dealing with common challenges

Unfamiliar words
- Solution:
  - Use context clues
  - Check modern versions
  - Focus on action words
  - Skip and come back

Complex plots
- Solution:
  - Track main story only first
  - Make character maps
  - Note key events
  - Use study guides

Long speeches
- Solution:
  - Break into sections
  - Find main ideas
  - Look for patterns
  - Read aloud

APPENDIX 1

Character Analysis Worksheet

Name: _____

Position/status: **Tragic flaw:**

    Celebrity   Pride

    Leader   Ambition

    Sports star   Jealousy

    Other: Anger

    Other:

Three personality traits:

1.

2.

3.

Bad decisions they make/made:

1.

2.

3.

Consequences of actions:

1.

2.

3.

APPENDIX 2

Historical Analysis Worksheet

Event/character: _____

Historical fact: _____

Shakespeare's version: _____

What changed?

_____

_____

Main character

_____

_____

Key battle

_____

_____

Important speech

_____

_____

Key relationship/s

_____

_____

APPENDIX 3

Sonnet Analysis Worksheet

Sonnet # _____

First quatrain (lines 1–4)
Main idea: _____
Rhyme pattern: _____
Key words: _____
Purpose of these lines: _____

Second quatrain (lines 5–8)
Development of idea: _____
Rhyme pattern: _____
Key words: _____
How does this build on the first quatrain? _____

Third quatrain (lines 9–12)
Further development: _____
Rhyme pattern: _____
Key words: _____
Any shift in thinking? _____

Couplet (lines 13–14)
Final message: _____
How does it conclude the sonnet?

_____

_____

APPENDIX 4

What; How; Why; So Analysis Worksheet

Character: _____
Scene: _____

WHAT (What exactly happens?)
_____

Quote to support:
_____

HOW (How does it happen?)
_____

Evidence in the text:
_____

WHY (Why does it happen?)
_____

Character's motivation:
_____

SO (So, what does this tell us?)
_____

Connection to themes:
_____

APPENDIX 5

Shakespeare transformed

Shakespeare's play	Modern adaptation
Romeo and Juliet	• *West Side Story* (1961, 2021) • *Romeo + Juliet* (1996) • *Gnomeo & Juliet* (2011)
Hamlet	• *Rosencrantz & Guildenstern Are Dead* (1990) • *The Lion King* (1994, 2019) • *Haider* (2014, Indian adaptation) • *Ophelia* (2018)
Macbeth	• *Throne of Blood* (1957, Akira Kurosawa) • *Scotland, PA* (2001) • *Macbeth* (2015) • *The Tragedy of Macbeth* (2021, Joel Coen)
The Taming of the Shrew	• *Kiss Me, Kate* (1948, musical adaptation) • *10 Things I Hate About You* (1999) • *Deliver Us from Eva* (2003, partial thematic adaptation)

Shakespeare's play	Modern adaptation
Twelfth Night	- *Twelfth Night*, or *What You Will* (1996) - *Illyria* (2002, musical adaptation) - *She's the Man* (2006)
Much Ado About Nothing	- *Much Ado About Nothing* (1993, Kenneth Branagh) - *Much Ado About Nothing* (2012, Joss Whedon)
Othello	- *Desdemona: A Play About a Handkerchief* (1979, Paula Vogel) - *"O"* (2001) - *Iago* (2016, play adaptation)
The Tempest	- *Forbidden Planet* (1956) - *The Island* (1973, Athol Fugard, South African adaptation) - *Prospero's Books* (1991) - *The Tempest* (2010, Julie Taymor)
King Lear	- *Ran* (1985, Akira Kurosawa) - *A Thousand Acres* (1997) - *King of Texas* (2002, TV movie) - *The Daughter* (2015, Australian adaptation)
Julius Caesar	- *Julius Caesar* (1953, classic Hollywood adaptation) - *Me and Orson Welles* (2008, includes Caesar production by Orson Welles) - *Caesar Must Die* (2012, Italian prison adaptation)

Shakespeare's play	Modern adaptation
A Midsummer Night's Dream	• *A Midsummer Night's Dream* (1999, Michael Hoffman) • *Shakespear Retold: A Midsummer Night's Dream* (2005, BBC adaptation) • *Were the World Mine* (2008, LGBTQ+ musical adaptation) • *Strange Magic* (2015)
The Merchant of Venice	• *Shylock is My Name* (1999, novel by Howard Jacobson) • *The Merchant of Venice* (2004, Al Pacino) • *Shakespeare Retold: The Merchant of Venice* (2005, BBC adaptation)
Richard III	• *Richard III* (1995, Ian McKellen) • *Looking for Richard* (1996, Al Pacino) • *House of Cards* (2013–2018, loosely inspired by themes of ambition and betrayal in *Richard III*)
Henry IV & Henry V	• *The King* (2019, Netflix adaptation of *Henry V*) • *My Own Private Idaho* (1991, partial thematic adaptation) • *Chimes at Midnight* (1965, Orson Welles)
Coriolanus	• *Coriolanus* (2011, Ralph Fiennes) • *An Enemy of the People* (modern adaptations borrowing themes)
Titus Andronicus	• *Tromeo and Juliet* (1996, campy modern reinterpretation blending *Titus* with *Romeo and Juliet*) • *Titus* (1999, Julie Taymor)

APPENDIX 6

Key words

General literary terms

Allusion	A reference to another text, historical event or cultural element
Antagonist	A character or force opposing the protagonist
Conflict	The central struggle in a story, whether internal (within a character) or external (between characters or forces)
Foreshadowing	Hints or clues about what will happen later in the story
Irony	A contrast between expectation and reality
Dramatic irony	When the audience knows something the characters do not
Situational irony	When events unfold differently than expected
Verbal irony	When words express the opposite of their literal meaning

Shakespeare-specific terms

Aside	A brief remark by a character meant to be heard by the audience but not by other characters
Couplet	Two consecutive rhyming lines in a poem, often concluding a sonnet
Hamartia	A tragic flaw or error in judgement leading to a character's downfall
Iambic pentameter	A poetic rhythm consisting of five pairs of stressed and unstressed syllables (da-DUM)
Protagonist	The main character in a story, often facing the central conflict
Quatrain	A stanza of four lines, often found in sonnets
Soliloquy	A speech where a character speaks their thoughts aloud, often when alone on stage

Key themes and ideas

Ambition	A driving force in characters like Macbeth, leading to both achievements and downfall
Appearance vs reality	A theme where things are not what they seem, as seen in *Macbeth* and *Twelfth Night*
Jealousy	A destructive emotion explored in *Othello*
Tragic flaw	A character trait leading to their downfall, such as Hamlet's indecision

Common Shakespearean words

Thou	You
Thee	You (object form)
Thy/thine	Your/yours
Art	Are
Anon	Soon
Hark	Listen
Prithee	Please
Wherefore	Why (not where)
Doth	Does

Analytical terms

Characterisation	How a character is developed through actions, dialogue and description
Imagery	Descriptive language appealing to the senses
Metaphor	A comparison between two things without using 'like' or 'as'
Motif	A recurring idea or symbol in a text
Theme	The central idea or message of a text
Tone	The author's attitude conveyed through language

Romances (late plays)

These are often considered a separate category combining elements of tragedy and comedy.

1. Cymbeline
2. The Tempest
3. Pericles, Prince of Tyre
4. The Winter's Tale
5. The Two Noble Kinsmen (attributed to Shakespeare and John Fletcher)

Sonnets

Shakespeare wrote 154 sonnets, which are traditionally grouped together as one collection. Here are the key themes:

- **Sonnets 1-17:** The Procreation Sonnets, urging a young man to marry and have children.
- **Sonnets 18-126:** Directed to a young man, discussing beauty, love and the passage of time.
- **Sonnets 127-152:** The Dark Lady Sonnets, exploring a more complex and sensual relationship.
- **Sonnets 153-154:** Classical allusions about love and lust.

Tragedies

1. Antony and Cleopatra
2. Coriolanus
3. Hamlet
4. Julius Caesar
5. King Lear
6. Macbeth
7. Othello
8. Romeo and Juliet
9. Timon of Athens
10. Titus Andronicus
11. Troilus and Cressida (sometimes classified as a problem play)

Histories

1. Henry IV, Part 1
2. Henry IV, Part 2
3. Henry V
4. Henry VI, Part 1
5. Henry VI, Part 2
6. Henry VI, Part 3
7. Henry VIII
8. King John
9. Richard II
10. Richard III

Complete list of Shakespeare's works

Comedies

1. All's Well That Ends Well
2. As You Like It
3. The Comedy of Errors
4. Cymbeline (sometimes classified as a romance or a tragedy)
5. Love's Labour's Lost
6. Measure for Measure
7. The Merchant of Venice
8. The Merry Wives of Windsor
9. A Midsummer Night's Dream
10. Much Ado About Nothing
11. Pericles, Prince of Tyre (sometimes classified as a romance)
12. The Taming of the Shrew
13. The Tempest
14. Twelfth Night
15. Two Gentlemen of Verona
16. The Winter's Tale (sometimes classified as a romance)

Introduction

I have a confession: I am not a fan of Shakespeare. This is a sacrilegious thing for an English teacher to say. I may get fired for immortalising these words in print!

Shakespeare can feel like a chore – trust me, I get it. But buried under all the 'thous' and 'thees' are stories packed with drama, humour, betrayal, situationships and big emotions. Things that hit hard today. This book is designed to cut through the jargon and show you how Shakespeare's plays and sonnets connect to the world in which you live.

I have tried to make this as accessible and relatable as possible – mainly for my own benefit! I have written this book with students in Years 7–10 in mind who have had one of The Bard's plays forced upon them. Once more unto the breach, dear reader.

Contents

Introduction		1
Complete list of Shakespeare's works		2
Chapter 1	Who was Shakespeare?	5
Chapter 2	Shakespeare's language	9
Chapter 3	Big ideas in Shakespeare's plays	17
Chapter 4	Shakespeare's comedies	23
Chapter 5	Shakespeare's tragedies	31
Chapter 6	Shakespeare's histories	39
Chapter 7	Shakespeare's sonnets	49
Chapter 8	Analysing Shakespeare's characters	59
Chapter 9	Adapting and transforming Shakespeare	69
Chapter 10	Tips for reading and enjoying Shakespeare	77
Appendix 1	Character Analysis Worksheet	81
Appendix 2	Historical Analysis Worksheet	82
Appendix 3	Sonnet Analysis Worksheet	83
Appendix 4	What; How; Why; So Analysis Worksheet	84
Appendix 5	Shakespeare transformed	85
Appendix 6	Key words	88

Note from the author:

Some of the images in this book are AI-generated.

Published in 2025 by Amba Press, Melbourne, Australia
www.ambapress.com.au

© Benjamin White 2025

All rights reserved. No part of this book may be reproduced or transmitted in any form or by any means, electronic or mechanical, including photocopying, recording or by any information storage and retrieval system, without prior permission in writing from the publisher.

Cover design: Tess McCabe
Internal design: Midlands
Editor: Rica Dearman

ISBN: 9781923215825 (pbk)
ISBN: 9781923215832 (ebk)

A catalogue record for this book is available from the National Library of Australia.

SHAKESPEARE SIMPLIFIED

Exploring the Bard's World
for Modern Students

BENJAMIN WHITE